OneNote 2016 - Taking Digital Notes

This manual is designed to document the features and capabilities of the installed version of **OneNote 2016** (not the online version) and includes the differences between **OneNote 2010** and **2013**. This is an electronic version of note-taking similar to using a **Notebook** binder. It is used for typing notes, collecting electronic information such as audio recordings, videos, electronic handwriting, pictures, email messages, Excel files, Word documents, etc. Once everything is organized, you can search for specific content. You can also **Tag** specific messages for quick recall using the search facility. As you attend meetings, or school lectures, or engage in internet research, you can type your notes, display pictures, and capture internet information electronically. This capability is available on **OneNote 2010**, **2013**, **2016**, and **Office 365 OneNote Online.**

Table of Contents

Student Projects

Exercise Download

Exercises are posted on the website and can be downloaded to your computer.
Please do the following:

Open Internet Explorer/Edge: Or Google Chrome:

Type the web address: **elearnlogic.com/download/onenote2016-a.exe**

You might get several security warnings, but answer yes and run through each one. When you click "**Unzip**," the files will be located in **C:\Data\OneNote2016-A** folder.

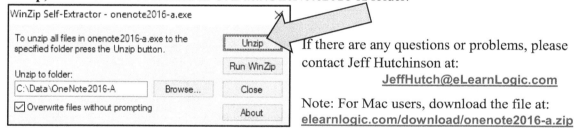

If there are any questions or problems, please contact Jeff Hutchinson at:

JeffHutch@eLearnLogic.com

Note: For Mac users, download the file at:
elearnlogic.com/download/onenote2016-a.zip

Copyright and Release Information

This document was updated on **6/23/2019** (Version 1), designed for **OneNote2013,** and updated for **OneNote 2016**. Also, it includes **OneNote 2010** features. However, this material is the sole property of **Jeff Hutchinson** and **eLearnLogic**. Any emailing, copying, duplication or reproduction of this document must be approved by **Jeff Hutchinson** in writing. However, students who take a class or purchase the material can use this document for personal development and learning. **ISBN:** 9781075768774

Chapter 1 - Interface and Basics

The **Interface** consists of **Notebooks, Sections** (folders), and **Pages**.

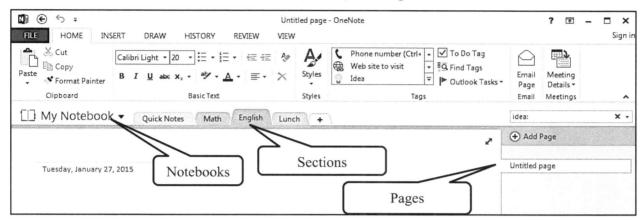

Section 1: File And Page Layout

Concept	Explanation / *Command String in italic.*
Practice Exercise 1	Exercise files on a **PC** are located at **C:\Data\OneNote2016-A** folder. Save all **Notebooks** in the folder **C:\Data\OneNote2016-A or C:\Data\OneNote2013-A** depending on the version of **OneNote** you are using. **Tip:** The **Mac** is usually stored in the download folder **OneNote2016-A**.
1.2 Notebook 2010	This is the **2010 Interface** located on the left side of the screen. It is used to navigate between **Notebooks**. The **Notebook** hierarchy is located on the left side of the screen and uses part of the workspace area.
Practice Exercise 2 *OneNote 2010* *Notebook*	1. *File Tab→New→Notebook* 2. *Enter the following:* **Store Notebook On:** *My Computer* **Name:** *OneNote Class* **Location:** *C:\Data\OneNote2010-A* *Choose*

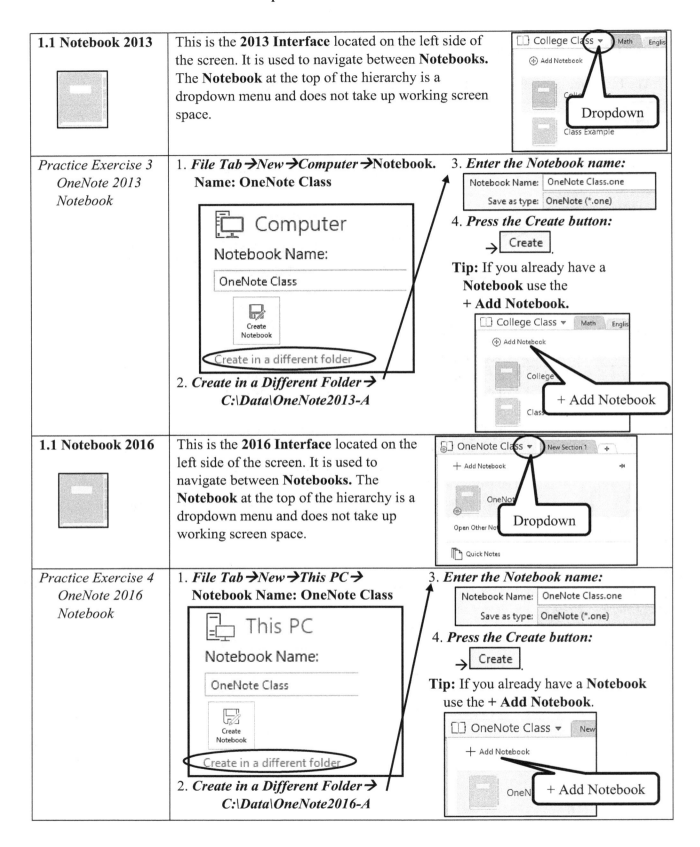

1.1 Notebook 2013	This is the **2013 Interface** located on the left side of the screen. It is used to navigate between **Notebooks**. The **Notebook** at the top of the hierarchy is a dropdown menu and does not take up working screen space.
Practice Exercise 3 OneNote 2013 Notebook	1. *File Tab →New →Computer →Notebook.* **Name: OneNote Class** 2. *Create in a Different Folder → C:\Data\OneNote2013-A* 3. *Enter the Notebook name:* 4. *Press the Create button:* **Tip:** If you already have a **Notebook** use the **+ Add Notebook.**
1.1 Notebook 2016	This is the **2016 Interface** located on the left side of the screen. It is used to navigate between **Notebooks.** The **Notebook** at the top of the hierarchy is a dropdown menu and does not take up working screen space.
Practice Exercise 4 OneNote 2016 Notebook	1. *File Tab →New →This PC → Notebook* **Name: OneNote Class** 2. *Create in a Different Folder → C:\Data\OneNote2016-A* 3. *Enter the Notebook name:* 4. *Press the Create button:* **Tip:** If you already have a **Notebook** use the **+ Add Notebook.**

Practice Exercise 5 *OneNote 2016* *OneDrive*	Some versions of **OneNote** require you to create the folder on **OneDrive** (the internet folder).. The following procedures will create ta **Notebook** on the **OneDrive** folder and then move it to a local folder.. 1. *File Tab→New→OneDrive→ Browse→* *Create a Folder called OneNote2016-A (Located in the OneDrive folder).* 2. *Enter the following:* 3. *Press the* Create *button.* 4. If the following message appears, Press: *Not Now.* 5. *The result should look similar to the following:* 6. **Move the OneDrive Notebook to a local drive:** *Right-Click on Notebook name→Properties→* *Change Location* Change Location... *→C:\Data\OneNote2016-A folder.* **The properties will look similar to the following:**

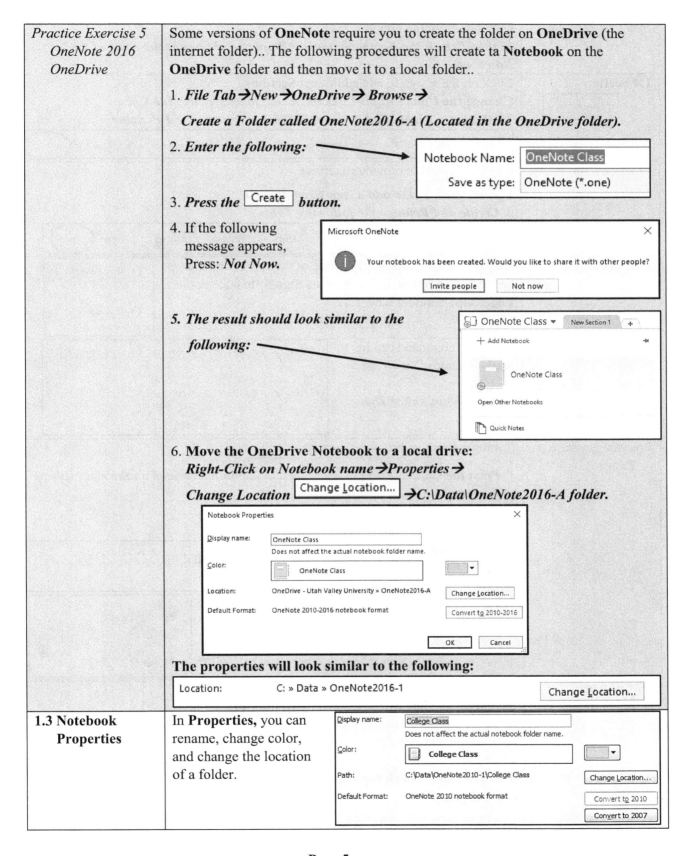

1.3 Notebook Properties	In **Properties,** you can rename, change color, and change the location of a folder.

Practice Exercise 6	Continue from the previous exercise. ***Right-Click on the Notebook name→Properties→Change the color of the Notebook.***
1.4 Section New Section	Click on the + sign to add additional **Sections**. **Change the Color:** *Right-Click on the tab to change the* **Tab Color.** **To Rename:** ***Right-Click or Double-Click to rename the*** **Tab name.** OneNote Class ▼ Home Formatting Insert Features Draw History Review View +
Practice Exercise 7	Continue from the previous exercise. 1. ***Press the*** + ***to add a New Section.*** 2. ***Create and Rename the following Tabs:*** Home Formatting Insert Features Draw History Review View +
1.5 Page	**Pages** are located on the right side of the screen and are tied to each **Section**. Click the **Plus Sign** + to add another **Page**. **Tip:** Shortcut Key: ***Ctrl N*** ⊕ Add Page Notes 2/2/2015 Notes 2/6/2015
1.6 Page Date	The **Date** command can be used to create a New Page. ***Insert Ribbon Tab → Date.*** ▦ Saturday, July 11, 2015 11:21 PM ◀ July, 2015 ▶ Su Mo Tu We Th Fr Sa 28 29 30 1 2 3 4 5 6 7 8 9 10 11
Practice Exercise 8 Page	Continue from the previous exercise. 1. ***Press the*** + Add Page ***button located on the right side of the interface.*** 2. **Enter a title:** ***Type: Notes*** 3. ***Insert Ribbon Tab →Date.*** Notes 6/20/2019 Thursday, June 20, 2019 7:59 PM 4. Review the pages on the right side of the interface: + Add Page Notes 6/20/2019
1.7 Subpage	**Subpages** are located under the **Pages** on the right side of the interface. They can be created by **Right-Clicking** on the desired **Page** and choosing **Subpage**. Note: **Page** 1 cannot be a **Subpage**. Create **Page** 2 and then **Right-Click** to create a **Subpage**. **Tip:** The **Spell Check** capability works the same for **Pages** and **Subpages**. + Add Page Notes 6/19/2019 Page1 Page2 Notes 6/20/2019

Practice Exercise 9 *Subpage*	***Continue from the previous exercise.*** ***Right-Click on the Page→Subpage→Page1.*** **Tip:** If the **Subpage** option is unavailable, create a **Page** first then create a **Subpage**.
1.8 Section **Groups**	For **Notebooks** that require many **Section Tabs** on top, a **Section Group** allows you to combine or group multiple **Sections** together. ***Right-Click*** ▰ New Section ▰ New Section Group

Practice Exercise 10
Section Groups
	1. ***Right-Click in the white space just above the Section names →***
	   New Section Group→Rename to Archive.
	2. ***Drag and drop Section Tab the New Section group.***
	
	View + ◢ Archive
	
	If you have 10 or more **Sections,** you need have to use the dropdown arrow ▱▾ .
	   Add several more sections to see the dropdown arrow:
	
	View New Section 1 New Section 2 New Section 4 ⋯ ▾

Student Project A - Create Notebook, Section, and pages

1. *Follow the practice exercises above to create a Notebook, section, pages and subpages.*

2. *Draw several containers or boxes on the page and type text in the container.*

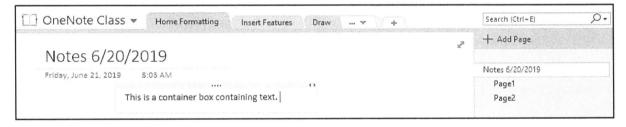

Section 2: Formatting Features

Formatting Tools are located in the **Home Ribbon Tab.**

OneNote 2013 Home Ribbon Tab

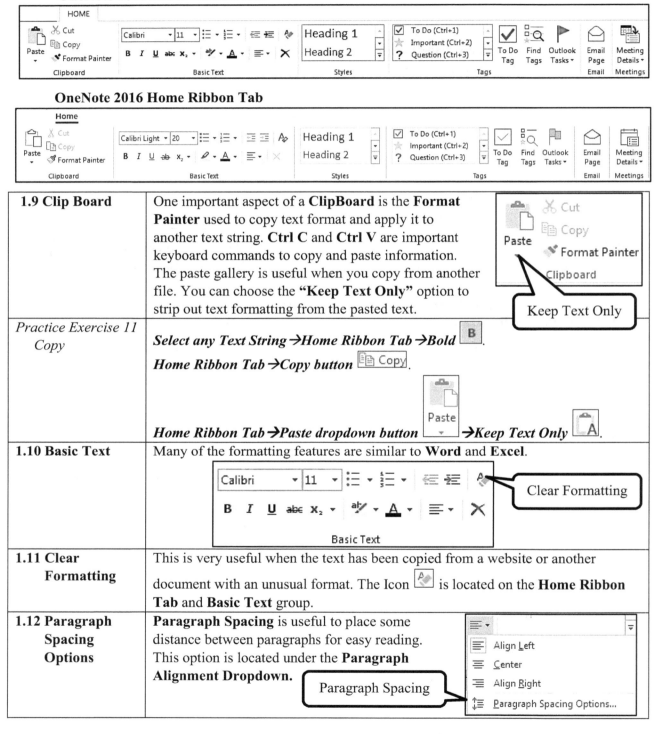

OneNote 2016 Home Ribbon Tab

1.9 Clip Board	One important aspect of a **ClipBoard** is the **Format Painter** used to copy text format and apply it to another text string. **Ctrl C** and **Ctrl V** are important keyboard commands to copy and paste information. The paste gallery is useful when you copy from another file. You can choose the **"Keep Text Only"** option to strip out text formatting from the pasted text.
Practice Exercise 11 *Copy*	***Select any Text String →Home Ribbon Tab →Bold*** B . ***Home Ribbon Tab →Copy button*** Copy . ***Home Ribbon Tab →Paste dropdown button*** Paste ***→Keep Text Only***.
1.10 Basic Text	Many of the formatting features are similar to **Word** and **Excel**.
1.11 Clear Formatting	This is very useful when the text has been copied from a website or another document with an unusual format. The Icon is located on the **Home Ribbon Tab** and **Basic Text** group.
1.12 Paragraph Spacing Options	**Paragraph Spacing** is useful to place some distance between paragraphs for easy reading. This option is located under the **Paragraph Alignment Dropdown.**

1.13 Styles	These are standard **Styles** similar to the ones located in **Microsoft Word. Tip:** You can't modify the **Style** sizes.	Heading 1 Heading 2 Styles

Section 3: Page Tags

Continue building **Pages** and testing the above features.

1.14 Tags	**Tags** are used to identify a specific **Container** (text box) to be used for search purposes. **Key Command: Ctrl 1-9.** The following are a few common **Tags**: 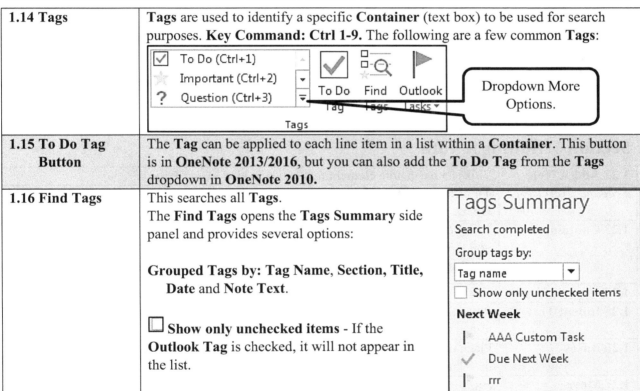
1.15 To Do Tag Button	The **Tag** can be applied to each line item in a list within a **Container**. This button is in **OneNote 2013/2016**, but you can also add the **To Do Tag** from the **Tags** dropdown in **OneNote 2010.**
1.16 Find Tags	This searches all **Tags**. The **Find Tags** opens the **Tags Summary** side panel and provides several options: **Grouped Tags by: Tag Name, Section, Title, Date** and **Note Text.** ☐ **Show only unchecked items** - If the **Outlook Tag** is checked, it will not appear in the list.

Section 4: Outlook Items

1.17 Outlook Tasks	This creates an **Outlook Task** that will link back to **OneNote.** **Tip:** The **OneNote 2010 Tags** are slightly different.
1.18 Outlook Tasks Unlinked	This adds a **Task** to **OneNote,** but is not **Linked** to **Outlook.** Click the flag to check off the task ✓ .

1.19 Outlook Tasks Linked Outlook Tasks	Choose the **Custom Option** to add a task that is **Linked** to **Outlook**. You must enter the **Task Subject** in both **OneNote** and **Outlook**. To open a task in **Outlook**: *Select task in OneNote→Outlook Tasks drop down→Open Task in Outlook.* ▶ Custom... (Ctrl+Shift+K) ✕ Delete Outlook Task Open Task in Outlook
1.20 Email Page Email Page Email	This opens the active **Page** in the body of **Email** message. However, the feature does not allow you to attach a **Section** or **Notebook**. The following is the created **Email Message**: 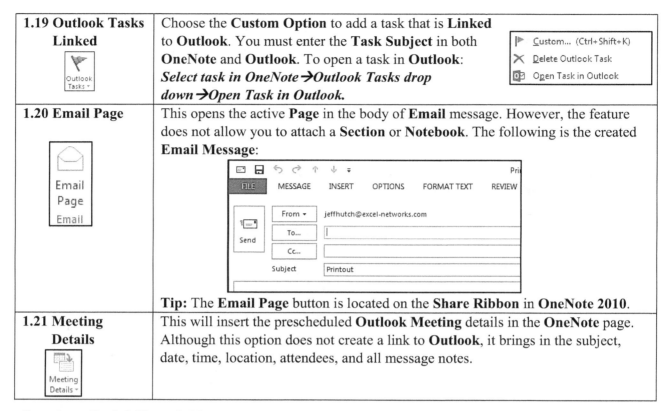 **Tip:** The **Email Page** button is located on the **Share Ribbon** in **OneNote 2010**.
1.21 Meeting Details Meeting Details	This will insert the prescheduled **Outlook Meeting** details in the **OneNote** page. Although this option does not create a link to **Outlook**, it brings in the subject, date, time, location, attendees, and all message notes.

Section 5: Adding A Note

1.22 Add A Note	This is a basic note element that can be added to any **Page**.
Practice Exercise 12	**To add a note to a Page:** *Select desired Page→Click on white space→Type: This is text.*
1.23 Container	Every object will be inside a **Container** that allows you to move things around. Grab the top portion of the **Container** in order to move it. Container
1.24 Expand Size	Click on the **Double-Arrow** to expand the size of the **Container Box**.
1.25 Indent Text	Place the **Cursor** in front of the text in the **Container** and press the **Tab** key to indent the text.
1.26 Boxes	Place the **Cursor** at the end of a text string and press the **Tab** key to add boxes to the **Container**.
1.27 Move Container	Click on the dots located on the top of a **Container** and move it.
1.28 Container Layering	**Containers** can be placed on top of one another to store more information in a viewable screen area. In some cases, one **Container** may be under a larger **Container**.
1.29 Mini Toolbar	**Right-Click** on selected text in a **Container** to see the **Mini Toolbar**. Calibri 11 B I U A Typed Text

Section 6: Section Options

1.30 Move Section,	To **Move** a **Section,** simply **Drag n Drop** to a different location.
Practice Exercise 13	*Click in the white area of the Page→Start typing a text string→Using your mouse grab the top portion of the Container→Move it to a new location.*
1.31 Section Color	*Right click on any Section tab→Section Color→(Choose Color).* 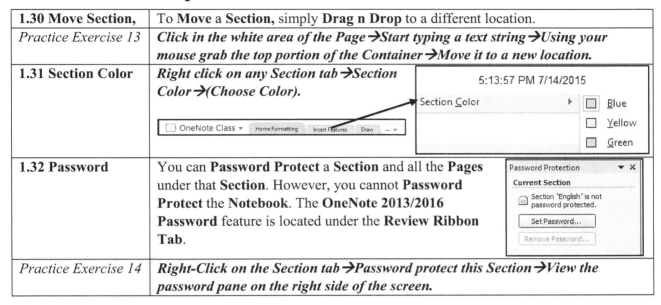
1.32 Password	You can **Password Protect** a **Section** and all the **Pages** under that **Section**. However, you cannot **Password Protect** the **Notebook**. The **OneNote 2013/2016 Password** feature is located under the **Review Ribbon Tab**.
Practice Exercise 14	*Right-Click on the Section tab→Password protect this Section→View the password pane on the right side of the screen.*

Section 7: File Tab

1.33 Send to Blog	**OneNote** will preview the **Page** in **Word** prior to sending to the blog **Page**. *File tab→Send→Send to Blog.*
1.34 Pinning	This will allow **OneNote** to remember a completed **Notebook**. *File Tab→Open→Click the pin located to the right side of the name.* 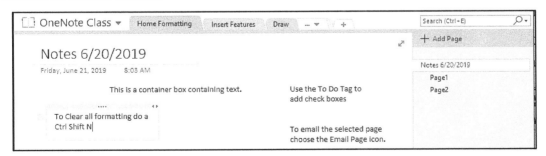
1.35 Auto Save	Notice the **Save** option is missing. That is because **OneNote** is always automatically **Saved**. To **Save** the entire **Notebook** to a different name, locate the folder and copy it to a new location.
1.36 Save As OneNote 2010	The **Save As** was initially used to save a **OneNote** notebook to a different folder. However, this feature was removed in **OneNote 2013**.

Student Project B - Document Features

Using the previous Student Project called **OneNote Class**, continue creating **Sections** and **Pages** to document all lessons learned.

Chapter 2 - Insert Ribbon Tab

In this chapter, we will insert objects into **OneNote**.

OneNote 2013 - Insert Ribbon Tab

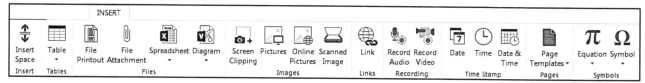

OneNote 2016 - Insert Ribbon Tab

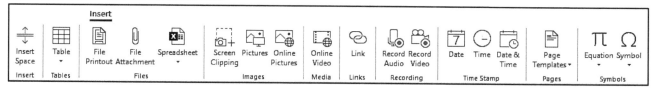

Section 1: Insert Files And Objects

Concept	Explanation / *Command String in italic.*
2.1 Insert Space Insert Space Insert	This **Inserts** a **Space** between two **Containers**. For example, if you create two **Containers** and stack them on top of each other, you can insert a **Space** between them (see **Container1** and **2** below). *Insert space button→Click in the middle between the Containers→Drag down.* Container1 Container2 **Tip:** This will separate **Containers** vertically but not horizontally.
2.2 Tables Table	The **Table** feature is similar to **Microsoft Word**. *Click the Tables dropdown arrow→drag to define your table size.* 3x2 Table
2.3 File Printout File Printout	This will open an application and then **Print** a document to **OneNote**. However, you cannot edit the text on top of the **File Printout Container**. It will **Print** the application **Page** to a default or an opened **OneNote Page**. The text in the image is searchable by the **Search** box located in the upper right corner.
Practice Exercise 15	***Open a blank OneNote Page→Insert Ribbon Tab→*** 🖺***File Printout→ Hawaii - Polihale Beach.docx→Insert.***

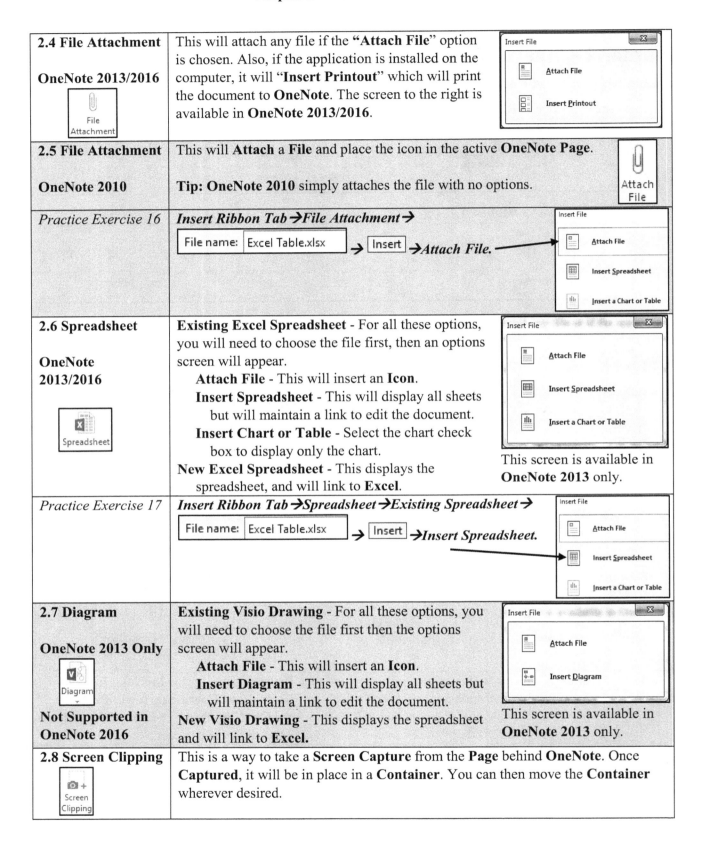

2.4 File Attachment **OneNote 2013/2016**	This will attach any file if the **"Attach File"** option is chosen. Also, if the application is installed on the computer, it will **"Insert Printout"** which will print the document to **OneNote**. The screen to the right is available in **OneNote 2013/2016**.	
2.5 File Attachment **OneNote 2010**	This will **Attach** a **File** and place the icon in the active **OneNote Page**. **Tip: OneNote 2010** simply attaches the file with no options.	
Practice Exercise 16	*Insert Ribbon Tab →File Attachment →* File name: Excel Table.xlsx → Insert →*Attach File.*	

2.6 Spreadsheet
 	
OneNote 2013/2016
	Existing Excel Spreadsheet - For all these options, you will need to choose the file first, then an options screen will appear.
	    Attach File - This will insert an **Icon**.
	    Insert Spreadsheet - This will display all sheets but will maintain a link to edit the document.
	    Insert Chart or Table - Select the chart check box to display only the chart.
	New Excel Spreadsheet - This displays the spreadsheet, and will link to **Excel**.
		This screen is available in **OneNote 2013** only.

Practice Exercise 17	*Insert Ribbon Tab →Spreadsheet →Existing Spreadsheet →* File name: Excel Table.xlsx → Insert →*Insert Spreadsheet.*	

2.7 Diagram
 	
OneNote 2013 Only
 	
Not Supported in OneNote 2016
	Existing Visio Drawing - For all these options, you will need to choose the file first then the options screen will appear.
	    Attach File - This will insert an **Icon**.
	    Insert Diagram - This will display all sheets but will maintain a link to edit the document.
	New Visio Drawing - This displays the spreadsheet and will link to **Excel**.
		This screen is available in **OneNote 2013** only.

2.8 Screen Clipping	This is a way to take a **Screen Capture** from the **Page** behind **OneNote**. Once **Captured**, it will be in place in a **Container**. You can then move the **Container** wherever desired.	

Practice Exercise 17	*Open a Web Page on the internet→Locate an object to be captured→Insert Ribbon Tab→ 📷 Screen clipping button→Draw a rectangle around the image to be captured.*
2.9 Pictures Pictures	This will insert a **Picture** from a file located on your local computer. Also, you can drag and drop a **Picture** from a desktop or browser to **OneNote**. **Tip:** This Icon is named "🖼 **Picture**" in **OneNote 2010**.
Practice Exercise 18	*Insert Ribbon Tab→ 🖼 Picture button→* *C:\Data\OneNote2016-A\Hawaii - Black Sand Beach.jpg→* Insert .
2.10 Online Pictures OneNote 2013/2016 Online Pictures	This will insert a **Picture** from a **SharePoint Server** folder or from a **Bing Image Search**. The screen to the right is available in **OneNote 2013/2016**. From SharePoint Browse content on your SharePoint sites Bing Image Search Search the web
2.11 Scanned Image Scanned Image	If a **Scanner Device** is installed in **OneNote,** it will control the scanner to merge an image to a **Page**. **Tip:** In **OneNote 2010,** the Icon is named **Scanner Printout.**

Section 2: Inserting Information

2.12 Link Link **OneNote 2016 Icon** 🔗	This will create a **Hyperlink** to a **Web Page** or **Page** in **OneNote**. The text will be displayed similar to a blue **Hyperlink** and will be placed in **OneNote**. To create a **Link:** *Insert Ribbon Tab→ Link* 🔗 *→* *Text to Display: (enter name).* **Option 1 -** In the address field type, a web address such as: http://www.elearnlogic.com **Option 2 - OneNote Link -** This will link to a specific **Page** in **OneNote**. *(Link dialog: Text to display; Address — Option 1; Or pick a location — Note: All Notebooks — College — Option 2)*
Practice Exercise 19	*Click on the Page area as if you were typing a text value→Insert Ribbon Tab→* *🔗Link button→Text to display: eLearnLogic* *Address:* www.elearnlogic.com
2.13 Record Audio Record Audio	This will **Record the Audio** of a class or meeting and the icon will be placed on an opened **Page**. You can also continue to take notes while it is **Recording**. 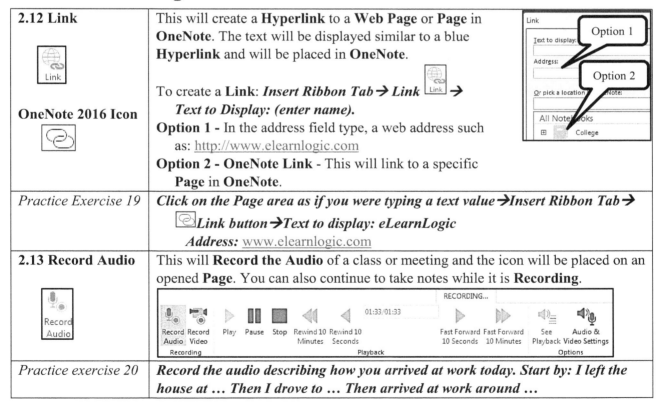
Practice exercise 20	*Record the audio describing how you arrived at work today. Start by: I left the house at … Then I drove to … Then arrived at work around …*

2.14 Record Video Record Video	This will **Record the Video** of a class or meeting and the icon will be placed on the opened **Page**. You can also continue to take notes while it is **Recording**. RECORDING... Record Audio	Record Video	Play	Pause	Stop	Rewind 10 Minutes	Rewind 10 Seconds	00:00/00:00	Fast Forward 10 Seconds	Fast Forward 10 Minutes	See Playback	Audio & Video Settings Recording · Playback · Options
2.15 Date Date	This will insert the **Date** to the location of the cursor. One technique is to insert the **Date** to define the **Page Name**. Example: Notes 2/2/2015.
2.16 Time Time	This will insert the **Time** to the location of the cursor.
2.17 Date&Time Date & Time	This will insert the **Date and Time** to the location of the cursor.
2.18 Equation Equation	This will insert a **Math Equation**. $A = \pi r^2$
2.19 Symbol Symbol	This will insert a **Special Character**. $+$ Ψ $\in$ $\pounds$ $¥$ $\copyright$ $\circledR$ TM $\pm$ $\neq$
2.20 Page Templates **OneNote 2013/2016**	You cannot apply a **Template** to an existing **Page** because the **Page Template** creates a **New Page**. However, you can apply a **Template** to a **Section,** but not a **Notebook**. You can also apply a **Section** as a default setting (see **Default Template**). Page Templates
Practice Exercise 21	**Identify and Select a Section→Insert Ribbon Tab→ Page Template→ (Choose a desired Template).** Test ▾ New Section 1 New Section 2 + Title Saturday, June 22, 2019 10:27 PM
2.21 Page Templates **OneNote 2010**	**Page Templates** are not available in the **Ribbons** but are available in the **Quick Access Toolbar**. *Quick Access Toolbar→Arrow →More Commands→ All Commands from: All Commands →Page Templates→Add.* Page Templates
Practice Exercise 21 OneNote 2010 Customize Ribbon	*File menu→Options→Customize Ribbon→ All Commands from: All Commands →Choose Page Templates→Add.* **Tip:** Verify where you are adding the **Page templates** button.

Student Project C - College Class

Create a new **Notebook** to record notes taken in a college class. There are files located in the **C:\Data\OneNote2016** folder that can be used to insert the appropriate material for each class.

1. *File Tab→New→Computer→Notebook Name: College Class.*

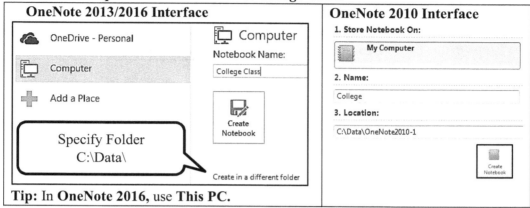

2. **Create Section Name: Math**

2a. **Create Page: Notes 2/5/18** (any date can be used)
   1. **Cut/Paste College Math problems:**
      In windows Open file→College Math Problems.txt.
   2. **Type text in a Container:** *Homework Assignment   1. 2. 3.* (see below)
   3. **Insert a To Do Tag:** *Select 1.2.3. → Home Ribbon Tab→Tag→To Do Tag.*

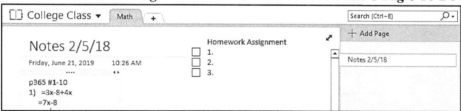

2b. Create Page: Notes 2/7/18 (any date can be used)

1. ***Insert Ribbon Tab*** ➔ ▯ ***File Attachment*** ➔
   C:\Data\OneNote2016-A\College Math Whiteboard.jpg.
2. ***Insert Ribbon Tab*** ➔ 🖾 ***Picture*** ➔
   C:\Data\OneNote2016-A\College Math Whiteboard.jpg.
3. **Type text in a Container:** ***Homework Assignment   1. 2. 3.*** (see below)
4. **Insert a To Do Tag:** ***Select 1.2.3.*** ➔ ***Home Ribbon Tab*** ➔ ***Tag*** ➔ ***To Do Tag.***

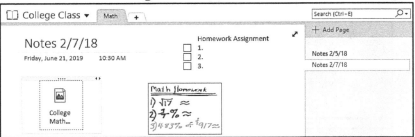

2c. Create Page: Notes 2/9/18 (any date can be used)

1. ***Insert Ribbon Tab*** ➔ 🖾 ***Picture*** ➔
   C:\Data\OneNote2016-A\College Math Ditosheet.jpg.
2. **Type text in a Container:** ***Homework Assignment   1. 2. 3.*** (see below)
3. **Insert a To Do Tag:** ***Select 1.2.3.*** ➔ ***Home Ribbon Tab*** ➔ ***Tag*** ➔ ***To Do Tag.***

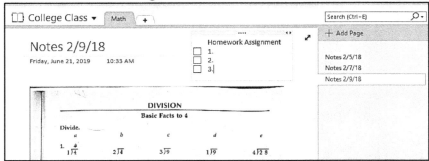

3. Create Section Name: English
    3a. Create Page: Notes 2/6/18 (any date can be used)
        1. *Insert Ribbon Tab→ Picture→*
        C:\Data\OneNote2016-A\College English Good Book.jpg.
        2. **Type text in a Container:** *Homework Assignment   1. 2. 3.* (see below)
        3. **Insert a To Do Tag:** *Select 1.2.3. → Home Ribbon Tab→Tag→To Do Tag.*

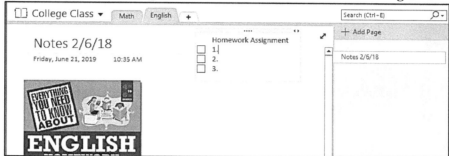

    3b. Create Page: Notes 2/8/18 (any date can be used).
        1. **Cut/Paste College English problems:**
        Open file: College English Grammer.txt.
        2. **Type text in a Container:** *Book Name: All About English.*
        3. **Select Text:** *All about English →Home Ribbon Tab→Tag→ Book to Read.*
        4. **Type text in a Container:** *Homework Assignment   1. 2. 3.* (see below)
        5. **Insert a To Do Tag:** *Select 1.2.3. → Home Ribbon Tab→Tag→To Do Tag.*
        Tip: Notice the **Pages** above are out of order. Reorder them.

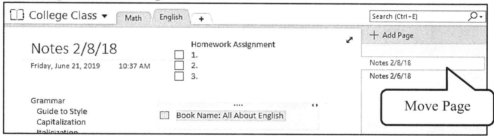

    3c. Create Page: Great Idea
        1. *Insert Ribbon Tab→ Picture→*
        C:\Data\OneNote2016-A\College English Order Now.jpg.

4. **Create Section Name: Science**
    4a. **Create Page: Notes 2/6/18** (any date can be used)

          1. *Insert Ribbon Tab→* 📎*File Attachment→College Science Experiement.mp4.*
          2. **Type text in a Container:** *Homework Assignment 1. 2. 3.* (see below)
          3. **Insert a To Do Tag:** *Select 1.2.3. → Home Ribbon Tab→Tag→To Do Tag.*

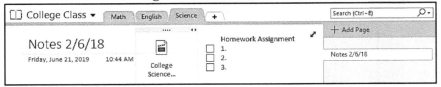

    4b. **Create Page: Notes 2/8/18** (any date can be used)

          1. **OneNote 2010:** Search the Internet for the keyword Science Projects and use 📷 **Screen Clipping** to capture the images found.

          2. **OneNote 2013/2016:** *Insert Ribbon Tab→* 🖼*Online Pictures→ Search: Science Project Ideas.*

Chapter 3 - Draw Ribbon Tab

This will allow you to use tools to **Highlight Text**.

OneNote 2013 - Draw Ribbon Tab

OneNote 2016 - Draw Ribbon Tab

Concept	Explanation / *Command String in italic.*
3.1 Type	This is the standard **Typing Mode** for text in order to create a text **Container**.
3.2 Lasso Select	This **Selects** objects by drawing a **Lasso** around the **Containers**.
3.3 Panning Hand	This will allow you to **Scroll** the **Page** up or down.
3.4 Eraser	This will **Erase** lines.
3.5 Drawing Tools	This will **Draw** a **Picture** using **Pen Tools,** or **Highlight Objects** using a **Highlighter.** More Drawing Tools
3.6 Colors & Thickness	This changes the **Color** of the active **Pen** or **Highlighter**.
3.7 Shapes	This adds **Shapes** similar to **Microsoft Word.** **Lock Drawing Mode** - This will allow you to draw several **Shapes** without re-clicking the **Shape** desired. **Snap to Grid** - This is used for a **Surface Pro Tablet** in order to write a smooth signature. Be sure to turn it off when finished.

3.8 Insert Space	This will **Insert** a **Space** between two **Containers**. Create two **Containers**, stack them on top of each other, and **Insert** a **Space** between them. This is the same as 2.1.	
Practice Exercise 22	*Insert Space button→click in the middle between the Containers and Horizontal tab→Drag down.*	
3.9 Delete	This **Deletes** an object. *Select the object→Delete button.*	
3.10 Arrange	This **Arranges** the stacking order of objects.	
3.11 Rotate	This **Rotates** an object.	
3.12 Ink to Text	If you use a **Pen** or **Stylus,** it will convert your writing to text. Use the **Drawing Tools** to convert words into text.	
3.13 Ink to Math	This converts your writing to typed characters.	
3.14 Math Operation	When you type a **Math Equation** in a **Container** and press = it will calculate the answer: Type the following: 5*2= Press the **Enter** key to finalize the equation.	5*2=10 5+2=7

Student Project D - Travel

1. *File Tab→New→Computer→Notebook Name: Travel*

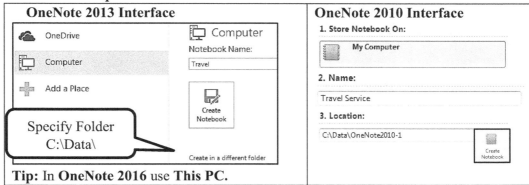

2. **Create Section Name: Travel Agent**

    2a. **Create Page: Agent Logo**

        1. *Open a Web Browser→Search for word: Travel Agent→*

        2. *Open OneNote→Insert Ribbon Tab→ Screen Clipping→Clip the Logo.*

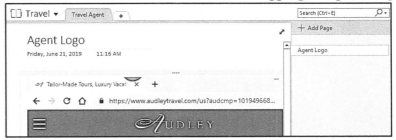

3. **Create Section Name: Hawaii**

    3a. **Create Page: Black Beach**

        1. *Insert Ribbon Tab→ Picture→*
           C:\Data\OneNote2016-A\Hawaii Black Sand Beach.jpg.

        2. *Insert Ribbon Tab→ File Printout→*
           C:\Data\OneNote2016-A\Hawaii Black Sand Beach.docx.

3b. Create Page: Polihale Beach

1. *Insert Ribbon Tab→Picture→*
   C:\Data\OneNote2016-A\Hawaii Polihale Beach.jpg.
2. *Insert Ribbon Tab→File Printout→*
   C:\Data\OneNote2016-A\Hawaii Polihale Beach.docx.

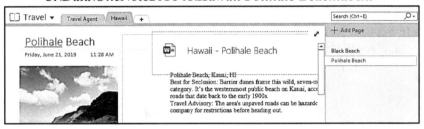

3c. Create Page: Wailea Beach

1. *Insert Ribbon Tab→Picture→*
   C:\Data\OneNote2016-A\Hawaii Wailea Beach.jpg.
2. *Insert Ribbon Tab→File Printout→*
   C:\Data\OneNote2016-A\Hawaii Wailea Beach.docx.

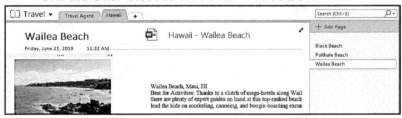

Chapter 4 - History Ribbon Tab

The **History Ribbon Tab** will keep track of **Page** versions and will have a date/author listed. You can click on any old version and see the results. **OneNote 2013/2016 (History Ribbon Tab)** and **OneNote 2010 (Shared Ribbon Tab)** names have changed, but the functionality is similar.

History Ribbon Tab (OneNote 2013)

OneNote 2013 - History Ribbon Tab

OneNote 2016 - History Ribbon Tab

OneNote 2010 - Share Ribbon Tab

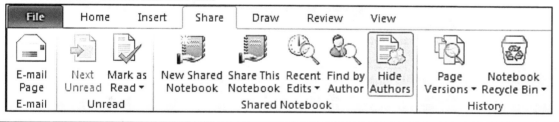

Concept	Explanation / *Command String in italic.*
4.1 Next UnRead	This will allow you to navigate through any **Unread Pages** or **Sections** to the next **Unread Page**. This option will help change the state of the **Pages** Read or Unread.
4.2 Mark As Read	The names of **Pages** with **Unread Notes** appear in bold letters. This helps to keep track of **Pages** you've read. Also, you can **Mark Notes** on a **Page** as **Unread** so that you can remember to revisit them later. This option will help change the state of the **Pages**.

Practice Exercise 23	1. ***Create a new Section→Create three new Pages and add text notes on each Page.*** 2. ***Make sure "✓ Show Unread Changes in This Notebook" is checked.*** 3. ***Select Page 1→Mark as unread→*** 4. ***Select Page 3→Mark as unread→Next Unread.***
4.3 Recent Edits	From this menu, choose the time frame of changes you want to view. You can view changes as **Recent** as today's changes or as far back as six months ago. The bottom option allows you to show **All Pages Sorted By Date**. Today... Since Yesterday... Last 7 Days... Last 14 Days... Last 30 Days... Last 3 Months... Last 6 Months... All Pages Sorted by Date...
4.4 Find By Author	This item will show the **Search Results** on the right sidebar. On the top of the **Search Field,** is a drop-down menu that allows you to change between searching the current **Section**, the **Section Group**, the entire **Notebook**, or all **Notebooks**. The **Sort By Author** drop-down menu below the search field allows you to sort results by date modified by author. A button to the right allows lets you choose whether to sort from **A-Z (Descending)** or from **Z-A (Ascending)**. Search Results Changes by Author Search All Notebooks Sort by Author Jeff Hutchinson Microsoft OneNote Basics 11/4/2013 OneNote: one place for al... 7/31/2012
4.5 Hide Authors	**Author** information will be **Hidden** when you select this option; select it again to show the information. When viewing **Authors**, you can see the initials of individual contributors.
4.6 Page Versions	This item lets you view all **Page Versions**, delete various configurations of **Page Versions**, or disable versioning history. **Page** versions are saved by date. However, if you modify the **Page** on the same date, it will not save two versions. Page Versions Delete All Versions in Section Delete All Versions in Section Group Delete All Versions in Notebook Disable History for This Notebook
Practice Exercise 24	***Right-Click on any Page→Show Page Versions.*** The versions are displayed under the **Page** name. Competency 4/5/2015 Jeff Hutchinson 4/2/2015 Jeff Hutchinson 3/24/2015 Jeff Hutchinson 3/23/2015 Jeff Hutchinson

4.7 Notebook Recycle Bin Notebook Recycle Bin	There is a separate **Recycle Bin** for each **Notebook** when a **Page** or **Section** is deleted. You can use the **Move** or **Copy** command to restore the **Page/Section** to its proper location. You can also **Empty** the **Recycle Bin**.	Notebook Recycle Bin Empty Recycle Bin Disable History for This Notebook
4.8 New Shared Notebook OneNote 2010 New Shared Notebook	This creates a **New Shared Notebook.** The button is available in **OneNote 2010.**	
4.9 Share This Notebook OneNote 2010 Share This Notebook	This shares an existing **Notebook**. The button is available in **OneNote 2010.**	
4.10 Email Page E-mail Page	The **Emails** the current **Page**. The button is located under the **Share Ribbon Tab** in **OneNote 2010** and in the **Home Ribbon Tab** in **OneNote 2013**.	

Student Project E - Personal Vacation

Research your favorite vacation destination. This will be your dream vacation so don't worry about money, time off work, or any other constraint. You decide how to categorize your **Sections** and **Pages**. It is important to be concerned about flight plans, maps, destinations, pictures, famous restaurants, family history, etc. Open a web browser and start your search. Use **OneNote** to organize your research for future reference.

File Tab→New→Computer→Notebook Name: Personal Vacation.

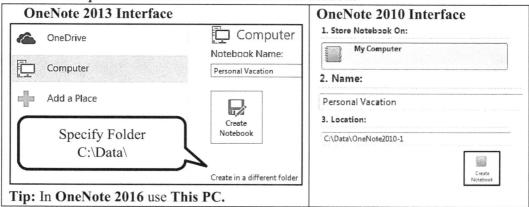

Chapter 5 - Review Ribbon Tab

This is primarily used for **Spell Checking.**

OneNote 2013 - Review Ribbon Tab

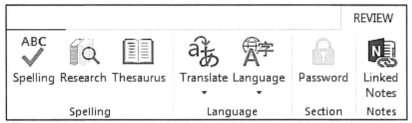

OneNote 2016 - Review Ribbon Tab

Concept	Explanation / *Command String in italic.*
5.1 Spelling 	This **Spell Checks** one page at a time unless you select specific text. Press **F7** to **Spell Check.**
5.2 Research 	This will **Research** reference material such as dictionaries and encyclopedias.
5.3 Thesaurus 	This will find related words for substitution. **OneNote 2013/2016.**
5.4 Translate 	This **Translates** into different **Languages**.
5.5 Language 	This changes **OneNote** to a different **Language.**
5.6 Section Password OneNote 2013/2016 	You can **Password Protect** a **Section** and all the **Pages** under the **Section**. However, you cannot **Password** protect the **Notebook**. Click the **Password** button in the **Review Ribbon Tab** and review the pane on the left side of the screen. To access the **Protection in OneNote 2010:** *Right-Click on the Section Tab→Password Protect This Section.*

5.7 Section Password **OneNote 2010**	You can **Password Protect** a **Section** or all **Sections** in **OneNote**. ***Right-Click on any tab→Password protect this Section.***	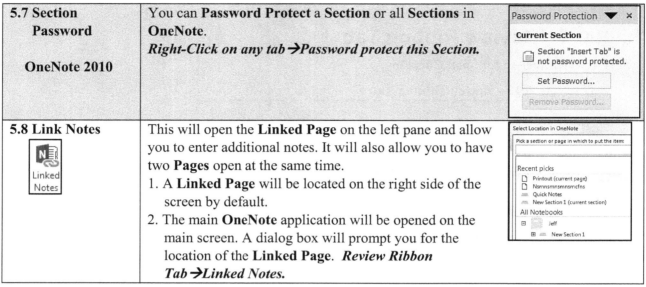
5.8 Link Notes Linked Notes	This will open the **Linked Page** on the left pane and allow you to enter additional notes. It will also allow you to have two **Pages** open at the same time. 1. A **Linked Page** will be located on the right side of the screen by default. 2. The main **OneNote** application will be opened on the main screen. A dialog box will prompt you for the location of the **Linked Page**. *Review Ribbon Tab→Linked Notes.*	

Student Project F - Spell Check a Document

1. **Create Section Name: Spelling   (any Notebook)**

    1a. **Create Page: File Printout**

    1. ***Insert Ribbon Tab→*** File Printout***→Spelling Practice.docx.***
    2. ***Review Ribbon Tab→Spell button.***

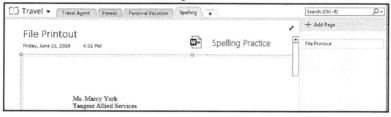

2a. **Create Page: Cut / Paste**

    1. **Microsoft Word:** *Open file Spelling Practice.docx→Select Text→Copy.*
    2. **Microsoft OneNote:** *Open OneNote→Locate Page called Cut/Paste→Paste.*
    3. ***Review Ribbon Tab→Spell button.***

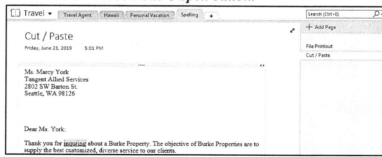

Conclusion: The File Printout feature did not allow **Spell Checking.**

Chapter 6 - View Ribbon Tab

The **View Ribbon Tab** is used for displaying **OneNote**.

OneNote 2013 - View Ribbon Tab

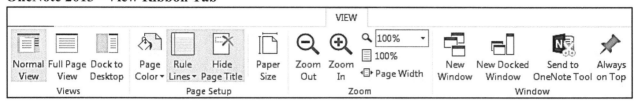

OneNote 2016 - View Ribbon Tab

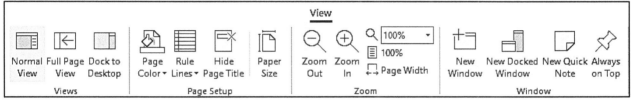

Concept	Explanation / *Command String in italic.*
6.1 Normal View	This is the regular layout. **Tip: In OneNote 2013/2016**, the left pane lists the opened **Notebooks**. If this is not available, click the **Down Arrow** ▼ then click the **Pin**.
6.2 Full Page View	This will not display **Ribbons** and **Page** panes. However, this view is ideal for note taking on a tablet. Click the **Double Angled Arrow** to return to normal mode. Also, the **Double Arrow** is located in the upper right corner of the document area.
6.3 Dock to Desktop	This will allow you to **Dock to Desktop** the **OneNote** window to the left or right side of the screen. This allows easy access to the **OneNote** application.
6.4 Hide Authors OneNote 2010 Only	**OneNote 2010:** The **Hide Authors** button is located in the **View Ribbon Tab**. **OneNote 2013/2016**: This is located in the **History Ribbon Tab**.
6.5 Page Color	This changes the background color of the active **Page**.

6.6 Rule Lines Rule Lines	This adds lines to the active **Page**. If you want the rule lines to appear on every new **Page,** choose: ✓ Always Create **Pages** with Rule Lines.	Rule Lines None Grid Lines Rule Line Color ✓ Always Create Pages with Rule Lines
6.7 Hide Page Title Hide Page Title	The **Page** title will be removed, and the topmost **Container** name will become the new name. However, the date stamp will be blank.	This will disappear Friday, March 13, 2015 9:05 AM
6.8 Paper Size Paper Size	This changes the **Printer Paper Size.**	
6.9 Zoom Out Zoom Out	This **Zooms Out.**	
6.10 Zoom In Zoom In	This **Zooms In.**	
6.11 Zoom 100% 100%	This **Zooms** to a set percentage of the screen.	110% 200% 150% 125%
6.12 Finger Zoom	If you are using a **Touchscreen** or **Tablet,** use your fingers on the screen to zoom.	
6.13 Page Width Page Width	This changes the **Page Width** of the working area. **OneNote 2013/2016.**	
6.14 New Window New Window	This opens the active **Notebook** in a **New Window** to allow you to see two **Sections** at the same time.	
6.15 New Docked Window New Docked Window	This **Docks** the active window on the left side of the screen.	

6.16 Send to OneNote Send to OneNote Tool	This opens the **Send to OneNote Tool**. It is **Supported in OneNote 2013/2016**.	*Send To OneNote*
6.17 New Side Note OneNote 2010 Only	This opens a new **OneNote Page** that can be saved to a new **Notebook**. **Tip:** This feature has been removed from the **OneNote 2013/2016** ribbon.	New Side Note
6.18 Always on Top Always on Top	This forces the active **Notebook** to be on top even if you switch to a different application. The **OneNote** will always remain on top of the desktop. You will need to minimize **OneNote** in order to see the application under the **OneNote** program.	

Student Project G - Staff Meetings

1. *File Tab→New→Computer→Notebook Name: Staff Meeting*

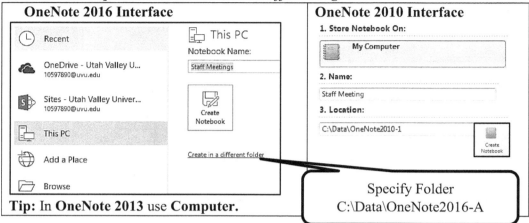

Tip: In OneNote 2013 use Computer.

2. **Create Section Name: Meeting Notes**

    2a. **Create Page: Meeting 2/12/18**

        1. *Home Ribbon Tab→Tag→Question (or keyboard command Ctrl 3)→*
           Type: *How do we build a better relationship with the IT department?*

        2. **Type text in a Container:** *Action Items 1. 2. 3.* (see below)

        3. **Insert a To Do Tag:** *Select 1.2.3.* → **Home Ribbon Tab→Tag→To Do Tag.**

        4. **2010:** *Insert Ribbon Tab→* File Printout→ *Visio FlowChart.vsd.*

           (If **Visio** is not installed use **Screen Clipping** on **Visio FlowChart.pdf**)

        5. **2013:** *Insert Ribbon Tab→Diagram→Existing Visio→Visio FlowChart.vsd.*

        6. **2016: Not supported**

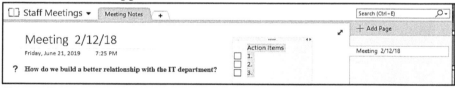

    2b. **Create Page: Meeting 2/19/18**

        1. **2010:** *Insert Ribbon Tab→* Attachment.

        2. **2013:** *Insert Ribbon Tab→* Spreadsheet→Excel Sheet1.xlsx→
           Sheet: Referral*

        3. **2016:** *Insert Ribbon Tab→* Spreadsheet→Existing Excel Spreadsheet→

           Excel Sheet1.xlsx → Insert → Insert Spreadsheet

        4. **Type text in a Container:** *Action Items 1. 2. 3.* (see below)

5. **Insert a To Do Tag:** *Select 1.2.3.* ➔ *Home Ribbon Tab ➔Tag➔To Do Tag.*

2c. **Create Page: Meeting 2/26/18**

1. **2010:** *Insert Ribbon Tab* ➔ *Attachment.*

2. **2013:** *Insert Ribbon Tab* ➔ *Spreadsheet➔Excel Multiple Sheets.xlsx➔ Calculation sheet*

3. **2016:** *Insert Ribbon Tab* ➔ *Spreadsheet➔Existing Excel Spreadsheet➔ Excel Multiple Sheets.xlsx* ➔ Insert ➔ Insert Spreadsheet

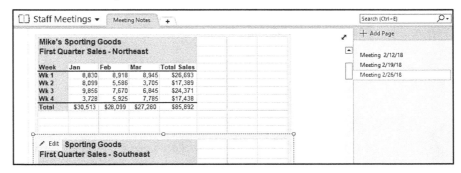

2d. **Create Page: Org Chart**

1. **2010:** *Insert Ribbon Tab* ➔ *File Printout➔ Visio Org Chart.vsd.*

   (If **Visio** is not installed use 🖼 **Screen Clipping** on **Visio Org Chart.pdf**)

2. **2013:** *Insert Ribbon Tab➔Diagram ➔Existing Visio* ➔ *Visio Org Chart.vsd.*

3. **2016:** *Insert Ribbon Tab* ➔ *File Attachment➔Visio Org Chart.vsd* ➔ Insert ➔ **Attach File**

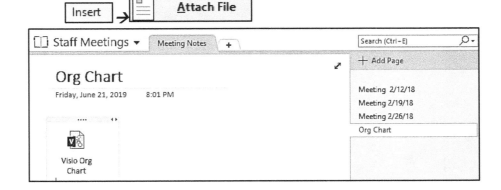

2e. **Create Page: Meeting 3/5/18**

    1. **2010:** *Insert Ribbon Tab* ➔ 📄*File Printout* ➔*Excel Chart.xlsx.*

    2. **2013:** *Insert Ribbon Tab* ➔ 📊 *Spreadsheet* ➔*Excel Chart.xlsx* ➔ *Calculation sheet.*

    3. **2016:** *Insert Ribbon Tab* ➔ 📊 *Spreadsheet* ➔*Existing Excel Spreadsheet* ➔

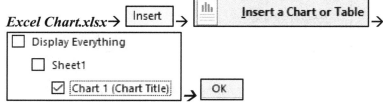

2f. **Create Page: Meeting 3/12/18**

    1. **2010/2013/2016:** *Insert Ribbon Tab* ➔📄*File Printout* ➔

    Excel Table.xlsx ➔ Insert

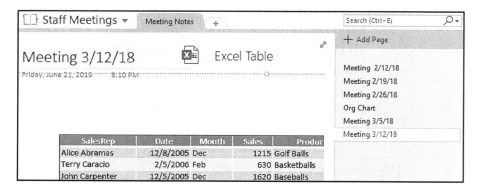

3. Create Section Name: Install Proposal

    3a. Create Page: Implementation Area

        1. Draw Ribbon Tab→Pen Tool→Use the Pen Tools.

        2. Draw Ribbon Tab→Insert→Shapes.

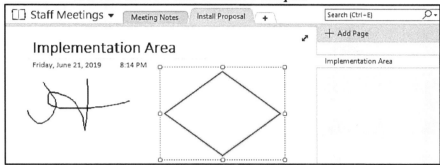

3b. Create Page: Proposed Facilities

3c. Create Page: Implementation Team

        1. Insert Ribbon Tab→ Link→ http://www.locations.com/

> Link   ✕
>
> Text to display:
>
> _____
>
> Address:
>
> http://www.locations.com

        2. Insert Ribbon Tab→ Table→5x5.

Chapter 7 - Advanced Topics

Section 1: Keyboard Shortcuts

7.1 Keyboard ShortCuts	Task Pane - Ctrl F1 Create Outlook Task 　　Ctrl Shift 1 to 5 Insert Hyperlink - Ctrl K Email Page - Ctrl Shift E Select Page - Ctrl Shift M Open Section - Ctrl O Create New Page - Ctrl N Next Section - Ctrl Tab Previous Section - Ctrl Shift Tab Open New Window - Ctrl M New Side Note Window 　　Ctrl Shift M Font Task Pane - Ctrl D	Cut - Ctrl X Copy - Ctrl C Paste - Ctrl V Bold - Ctrl B Italics - Ctrl I Underline - Ctrl U Spell Check - F7 Print - Ctrl P Undo - Ctrl Z Redo - Ctrl Y Help - F1 Full Page - F11	**Tag Shortcuts** ☑ To Do (Ctrl+1) ★ Important (Ctrl+2) ? Question (Ctrl+3) Remember for later (Definition (Ctrl+5) ✐ Highlight (Ctrl+6) ▤ Contact (Ctrl+7) ⌂ Address (Ctrl+8) ☎ Phone number (Ctrl+9)

Section 2: General Features

7.2 Search	You can search an entire **Notebook** for any text printed to **OneNote**. Search (Ctrl+E)　　　　🔍 ▾
Practice Exercise 25	1. ***Create a New Section: Click the* ⊕ →*Rename it to Search.*** 2. Print the following to a new **Page** for each item: 　　***Click*** ⊕ Add Page →***Insert Ribbon Tab*→*File Printpout*→** 　　　　Hawaii - Black Sand Beach.docx 　　　　Hawaii - Polihale Beach.docx 　　　　Hawaii - Wailea Beach.docx 3. ***Use the search feature to find specific text in the documents.*** 　　Beach|　　　　　　　× ▾
7.3 Search Graphics	There is a feature that allows the search capability to find words in a graphic image. However, it doesn't work well. **Tip:** Make sure the option is turned on: *File Tab→Options→Advanced Tab→* 　　Text recognition in pictures 　　☐ Disable text recognition in pictures **Test It:** Insert the images Washington.jpg, .gif, .png, and .tif.

7.4 Quick Notes **??Reread**	**Quick Notes** is located where a **Notebook** is opened. Information is printed and saved that forms external programs such as web browsers. If **OneNote** needs to store captured information and does not know where to place it, the information will be placed it in the **Quick Notes** area.	2010 Unified Notes Notebooks: ‹ 📓 Test Notebook ︿ 📄 New Section 1 📚 Unfiled Notes The feature was called Unified Notes in **OneNote 2010.**	2013/2016 Quick Notes ⊕ Add Notebook Meetings Open Other Notebooks 📑 Quick Notes

7.5 Touch Mode **OneNote 2013/2016**	The screen can be laid out in **Tablet Touch Mode** or **Mouse Mode**. *Quick Access* *drop down* ⇒ ✓ Touch/Mouse Mode *→Click on icon* *→Choose* Touch More space between commands. Optimized for use with touch.
7.6 Default Template	You can specify a **Default Template** layout for all new **Pages** in each **Section**. Always use a specific template Pick a template you want to use for all new pages in the current section. No Default Template ▾
Practice Exercise 26	***Insert Ribbon Tab→Page Templates→See pane on the left side of the screen (lower portion of the screen).***
7.7 Template Creation	If you have a specific **Page** layout (containing text notes and objects), you can create a custom template. This will be added to the **Template** area called **My Template** list. Create new template Save current page as a template Set up the **Page** desired and create a new template.
Practice Exercise 27	1. ***Create a new Page→Add a note called "Enter Notes Here."*** 2. ***Create an actions list called "Action List" and add ToDo boxes in the front.*** 3. ***Apply your favorite template to the Page→Insert Ribbon Tab→ Page Templates→See pane on left side of screen/lower portion of the screen.*** 4. ***Save current Page as a template→Template name: "My New Action Page."***
7.8 Office Theme	**OneNote 2013/2016.** *File Tab→Account→Office Theme.*
7.9 Version	**OneNote 2013/2016.** *File Tab→Account→Office Theme.*
7.10 Customized Ribbon	*File Tab→Options→Customized Ribbon.*
7.11 Quick Access Toolbar	This can be accessed from the **Options**. 📘 ⊙ ↺ ⇒ **Tip:** For **OneNote 2010,** the **Page Template** feature should be added.
Practice Exercise 28	***File Tab→Options→Quick Access Toolbar→All Commands→Select desired command→Add→Ok.***
7.12 Custom Tag	Create a custom Tag. *Home Ribbon Tab→Tag Dropdown→Custom Tag.*

Section 3: External Programs

7.13 Export	This will **Export** a **Page**, **Section** or entire **Notebook** to an external file. *File tab→Export.* Tip: **OneNote 2010** uses the name "**Save As**" to export information. *File tab→Save As*
7.14 Backup Location	This will allow you to define the location of your **Backups**. You can specify **Backups** to run automatically. *File Tab→Options→Save & Backup.*
7.15 Send To OneNote	**Open the application called "Send to OneNote 2013." (or 2016)** **Screen Clipping (Ctrl 5)** - This will ask where to save the clip each time. **Send to OneNote (Ctrl D)** - In Word, it will send the entire **Page** and create **Subpages** if the document has multiple **Pages**. **New Quicknote (Ctrl N)** - This will create a new blank **Notebook**.
7.16 Clipper For IE	This is an add-on program used for **Browsers**. It is used to capture the entire **Web Page** and place it in **OneNote**. 1 - *Open Internet Explorer→Tools ⚙ →Manage Add-ons→Toolbars and Extensions→Select Send to OneNote→Enable.* 2. *Right-Click on top of IE→Command Toolbar:* 3. *Use the following Icons to capture the website:* .

Section 4: Share Capabilities

7.17 Share Drive	If the folder is located on a **Shared Drive,** everyone with access can view the information. You may need to **Password Protect** the **Sections**.
7.18 Cloud	This is the **OneDrive Folder** or **Sharepoint** server.
7.19 Move Notebook	This will **Move** an entire **Notebook** to a specified destination. **OneNote 2010** and **2013/2016** handle the **Move** slightly different, but the result is the same. *File Tab→Share.*
7.20 General Options	*File Tab→Options→General Tab.*
7.21 Display Options	*File Tab→Options→Display Tab.*

7.22 Proofing	*File Tab→Options→Proofing.*	**AutoCorrect options** Change how OneNote corrects and formats text as you type: [AutoCorrect Options...] **When correcting spelling in Microsoft Office programs** ☑ Ignore words in UPPERCASE ☑ Ignore words that contain numbers ☑ Ignore Internet and file addresses ☑ Flag repeated words ☐ Enforce accented uppercase in French ☐ Suggest from main dictionary only [Custom Dictionaries...] French modes: [Traditional and new spellings ∨] Spanish modes: [Tuteo verb forms only ∨] **When correcting spelling in OneNote** ☑ Check spelling as you type ☐ Hide spelling and grammar errors ☑ Check grammar with spelling
7.23 Save & Backup	*File Tab→ Options→Save & Backup.*	**Save** Quick Notes Section C:\Users\Jeff Hutchinson\Documents\OneNote Notebooks\Personal\Unfiled Notes.on Backup Folder C:\Users\Jeff Hutchinson\AppData\Local\Microsoft\OneNote Default Notebook Location C:\Users\Jeff Hutchinson\Documents\OneNote Notebooks [Modify...] **Backup** ☑ Automatically back up my notebook at the following time interval: [1 Week ∨] ☑ Back up notebooks stored on SharePoint Number of backup copies to keep: [2] [Back Up Changed Files Now] [Back Up All Notebooks Now] **Optimizing files** Percentage of unused space to allow in files without optimizing: [15%] ☑ Optimize files after OneNote has been inactive for the following number of minutes: [20] [Optimize All Files Now] **Cache file location** Modifying the OneNote cache file location is not recommended. Any unsynced changes will be lost. It should only be modified if you need to move it to a disk with more space. It should always be on a non-removable hard disk in a secure location that is not accessed by other programs or users. Path: [C:\Users\Jeff Hutchinson\AppData\Local\Microsoft\OneNote] [Modify...]
7.24 Send To OneNote	*File Tab→Options→Send To OneNote.*	**Outlook Items** Email messages: [Always ask where to send] Meeting notes: [Always ask where to send] Contact notes: [Always ask where to send] Task notes: [Always ask where to send] **Other Content** Web content: [Always ask where to send] Print to OneNote: [Always ask where to send] Screen clippings: [Always ask where to send]

7.25 Audio & Video	*File Tab→Options→Audio & Video.*	Audio & Video
		When playing linked audio and video, rewind from the start of the par seconds:
		Audio recording settings:
		Device: Default Device
		Input: Master Volume
		Codec: Windows Media Audio Voice 9
		Format: 12 kbps, 16 kHz, mono
		Video recording settings:
		Device: Default Device
		Profile: Windows Media Video 9 for Local Area Network (256 Kbps)

Student Project H - Optional Projects
Other types of projects that can be created:

- Recording receipts
- Research projects
- Family pictures
- Genealogy history
- Planning a major vacation
- Meeting notes
- School class notes
- Evaluating a software package

About the Author

Jeff Hutchinson is a computer instructor teaching a variety of classes around the country. He has a BS degree from BYU in Computer-Aided Engineering and has worked in the Information Technology field supporting and maintaining computers for many years. He also previously owned a computer training and consulting firm in San Francisco, California. After selling his business in 2001, he has continued to work as an independent computer instructor around the country. Jeff Hutchinson lives in Utah and also provides training for Utah Valley University Community Education system, offering valuable computer skills for the general knowledge of students, career development, and career advancement. Understanding the technology and the needs of students has been the basis for developing this material. **Jeff Hutchinson** can be contacted at JeffHutch@elearnlogic.com or **(801) 376-6687.**

Workbook Design And Organization

Workbook Design

This workbook is designed in conjunction with an **Online-Instructor-Led course** (for more information see: **www.elearnlogic.com**). Unlike other manuals, you will not need to review lengthy procedures in order to learn a topic. All that is needed are the brief statements and command paths located within the manual that demonstrate how a concept is used. Furthermore, you will find that this manual is often used as a reference to help understand concepts quickly, and an index is provided on the last **Page** of the manual to reference **Pages** as necessary. However, if more detail is needed, you can always use the Internet to search for a concept. Also, if your skills are weak due to lack of use, you can refresh your memory quickly by visually scanning the concepts needed and then testing them out using the application.

Workbook Organization

The following are special formatting conventions:

Numbered Sections on the left are the **Concepts** covered.

Italic Text is used to highlight commands that will perform the concept or procedure in completing the practice exercises.

Practice Exercises are a **Step-by-Step** approach to demonstrate the concept.

Student Projects are a more comprehensive approach to demonstrate the concept.

Dark, Grayed-Out Sections are optional/advanced concepts.

Bolded items are commands in the ribbons or commands used.

Tip - These are additional ideas about the concept.

OneNote 2016 Index